NATIONAL
GEOGRAPHIC

Everything Is Made of Matter

Cypress Hills Community School / P.S. 89

265 Warwick Street

Brooklyn, New York 11207

Rowan Sellers

Contents

Everything Is Matter

What is matter?

Matter is anything that takes up space.

Even people are made of matter!

States of Matter

Matter exists in different forms, or states. The three most common states of matter are solid, liquid, and gas.

A pebble is a solid.

Water is a liquid.

Bubbles of air are gas.

Food

All the food in our kitchens is matter.

Sometimes we heat food.
Heating can make matter change
from one state to another state.

Solid butter melts when it is heated.
It becomes a liquid.

Sometimes we freeze food.
Freezing can make matter change
from one state to another state.

When you freeze juice, it becomes hard.
It becomes a solid.

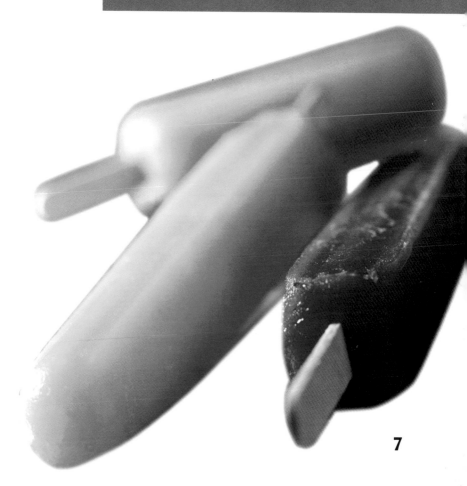

Fizzy Drinks

Drinks are liquids.

A liquid takes the shape of its container.

Some drinks have bubbles of gas in them.

If you leave a fizzy drink sitting out without a cap on it, all the gas escapes.

The drink in the open bottle doesn't have bubbles in it anymore.

Things Filled with Air

Air is a gas. It is all around us.
Some things that we use
need to have air inside them.
The air spreads out and fills them.

Tires need to be filled with air to roll along smoothly.

When we blow up a balloon,
we are putting air into it.

Up, Up, and Away

Air and other kinds of gases can make balloons float into the sky.

These balloons are filled with a special gas called helium. Helium is lighter than air, so the balloons rise.

The air inside these hot-air balloons is heated by gas burners.

The warm air inside the balloons is lighter than the cooler air outside, so the balloons rise.

13

From Wet to Dry

Where does the water go
when wet clothes dry?
Where does the water go
when a puddle disappears?

These T-shirts are drying in the sun.
Heat from the sun changes water
into a gas, which is called water vapor.

As this puddle dries, we can see the water turning into water vapor. The water is changing state from a liquid to a gas.

Cold Weather

What happens to matter
when the weather is very cold?